D1169789

Praise *for* *Creating Urgency*
in a Non-Urgent Housing Market

"This book is right on target! Its hard-hitting message delivers the details of the new mindset needed to succeed in this downside market."

DAVE McKOWN, Director of Sales and Marketing
Northern California Region
William Lyon Homes

"*Creating Urgency in a Non-Urgent Housing Market* hits home regarding the challenges we face in today's market. It inspires sales professionals to empower themselves to take action and eliminate excuses. It promotes the idea that success is achievable in any market. The book is clear, to the point and there is no mistaking its message—it's not the market, it's not the price, it's about you and the actions you take to improve someone's life by helping them into a home. My team was left challenged and inspired by its contents. In addition to myself, other managers within the organization view the new home sales market in a completely different way after reading this book."

KELLY RAE, Director of Sales and Marketing
ColRich Homes, San Diego

"*Creating Urgency* is an easy-to-read, straightforward look at selling homes in today's challenging market. It presents tools to create sales strengths for lasting ability. Jason says, 'When you change the way you look at selling, selling changes. When you change the way you look at yourself, you will change.' This mentality has assisted us in becoming the #1 team in unit volume for our company across the nation. Jason presents in these pages a map that, if followed, can create immediate improvements in selling results. I am excited about our continued success using these tools."

SUSAN LEE, New Home Manager
Richmond American Homes, Las Vegas

CREATING URGENCY

in a NON-URGENT HOUSING MARKET

Jason Forrest

www.JasonForrestSpeaker.com

Third edition, printed May 2010.

© 2007, 2008, 2010 by Jason Forrest

All rights reserved. No part of this book may be reproduced, transmitted, or stored in any form or by any means whatsoever without express written permission in advance from the author, except in the case of brief quotations in critical articles and reviews.

For information or bulk orders, contact:

info@shoreforrest.com

Printed by Branch-Smith Printing.

Fort Worth, Texas

International Standard Book Number: 0-9801762-1-2 (10 digit)

978-0-9801762-1-6 (13 digit)

Contents

Acknowledgements

To all of my family and friends who have been a part of my life and have believed in me, you have imparted your wisdom upon me, and for that I am grateful.

To my father, who has been selling his whole life, you have taught me what being a "salesperson" really means. To my mother, thank you for being the greatest teacher that I have ever known.

To Richard Tiller, whose revolutionary ideas from *Selling With Momentum* inspired me to write this book.

To Kara Libick, who has endured many sleepless nights working to help bring my concepts to life.

To Jeff Shore, who put his reputation on the line by entrusting me with his company. Thank you for being the best example of a "world class trainer" to follow.

To my wife, Shelly. I thank God for you everyday, and that you chose me. I love you, and this book is dedicated to you.

If you **REMEMBER**

NOTHING ELSE *from this* **BOOK,**

REMEMBER *these* **TWO TRUTHS:**

1

A person's desire to improve their life has more
influence over their buying decision than
any other factor.

2

Your ability to make greater income in today's
market is not a matter of chance, but it is a
matter of choice. The choices you make each
week decide your future—not any other factor.

We cannot allow ourselves

to be

victims of circumstance.

1

RECLAIMING

Our

HOPE

"Market projections bleak."

"Some homebuilders nearing bankruptcy."

"Next year will be tougher."

The 2007 headlines were enough to shake even the most experienced new home sales counselor to the core. Yet in sales offices, hallways and break rooms across America, one could hear the chatter of veiled optimism: **"We'll weather this storm,"** or, "That's how the industry is—up and down… we've just gotta sit tight and wait for the upswing."

But behind their masks of confidence, those sales counselors were wrestling with pressure, anxiety and dread. Everyone in the industry—from the builders to the sales teams, from the contractors to the lumberyard workers—everyone felt stress. Their once-reliable financial pipeline was drying up, and they felt powerless to do anything to stop the damage it was causing not only to their companies, but also to their personal lives.

For sales counselors who are dependent upon sales for their income, difficult years take an emotional toll. When their paycheck is slim, they have to drive home and tell their family that Christmas will be a little lean this year, or that they'll have to skip the summer vacation. For some, the situations are more serious—defaulted school loans, credit card debt, loss of health insurance or failure to pay their own mortgages. These are the real headlines, stories that reflect the struggle of men and women who grew accustomed to living on the success of years like 2004, and now must adjust to the realities of a tough market.

Most of us have grown to tolerate the ups and downs of the market. **We've accepted that we are in an industry that allows its success to be controlled by circumstances.** In hot markets that isn't much of a problem—we have circumstances such as more demand than supply, low interest rates, or mortgages handed out to people with FICO scores of 20. But when we rely on those kinds of circumstances to create our success, we create a problem for ourselves. The problem is that, **in tough markets, we suffer because those positive circumstances don't exist anymore.** Supply outnumbers demand, interest rates increase and homeowners experience the fallout from those subprime mortgages.

Where does that leave us? Well, **if we don't change our tactics, if we don't make improvements in the way we sell homes, we will not make great money until the next great housing market comes along.**

I don't know about you, but I don't enjoy placing my life in the hands of a market, an industry or numbers ticking across the bottom of the television screen. I don't want to listen to media reports that tell us we have no hope. That is why I have written this book. I want you to know that it doesn't have to be this way.

When you walk into your sales meeting and **your manager asks, "How many sales are you going to make this week?"** you don't have to fumble for an answer—you can *know* it. You can take control of your income, your success and your life. How? By tapping into the power of urgency.

True urgency is a person's desire to improve their life. This desire has more influence over a person's buying decision than any other factor. Forget the market conditions. Forget the negative reports in the media. People buy homes because they want to improve their lives. This very truth is what gives you the power to overthrow the circumstances of markets like 2008, and this book is intended to show you how.

Choose to Take Control

What I've said so far might be tough to accept at face value. It is certainly true that crumbling markets hurt sales. I'm not denying that. But, **we have a choice as to how we handle our circumstances.** And right now our industry is making the choice to let circumstances run the show. This acceptance of market cycles enables organizations to pass the blame, to point fingers at the market when profits fall.

When it comes down to it, **our industry suffers from a worth issue.** Builders everywhere are so used to living at the mercy of the market cycle that they have accepted that the worth of their homes is dependent upon outside factors. They choose to believe that **their success is not in their hands**. This worth issue spreads through every organization, affecting the way sales managers and their teams do business.

In 2007 I had countless managers show me their numbers, and then defend themselves and their team by blaming the market. They would say things like, "Well, it's just a really tough market right now," or, "You know, it's bad now, but things will get better when the market picks back up." They think they're doing their team a favor, that they're helping to encourage them. But what they don't realize is that comments like these help to make a bad situation worse.

When a manager tells their sales counselors that poor sales numbers are due to the market, they're communicating that great profits only happen because of great markets—not because of great sales counselors. Therefore, sales counselors begin to believe that they don't factor into the equation, that they don't make a difference. They begin to think that they have no influence in someone's decision to buy a home. If success only comes from great markets, then why should they bother to improve their sales skills? Why go to training? Why be coached? Why should they attempt to make a difference?

Do you see what's happening? Are you starting to put the pieces together? Our industry's resignation to circumstance trickles down through each individual organization, reinforcing the belief that market circumstances determine success. This victim mentality then cripples the self-worth of our sales teams. Sales counselors and managers lose their belief in themselves and they lose their desire for improvement. After all, why challenge the market when you've been told that it's a losing battle? **When sales teams feel powerless to change their circumstances, their only hope is that the market will improve.** Each month they look at their diminishing paycheck and wonder, "When will things get better?" They grow weary of the market controlling their destiny and their success.

My wife and I are fans of a movie called *Facing the Giants*. It is a story of a small private school football team that just couldn't seem to win a game. They couldn't catch a break. ***Even worse, they had already written off the thought of winning a game because they had lost hope in themselves.*** However, as their coach helped to restore their confidence and courage, their lives and their game transformed. They felt powerful enough to face the giants in their lives—both on and off the field—and they rose to win in spite of the odds stacked against them. Their newfound hope in themselves was the wild card that made it all possible.

Just as the team in this story lost hope, I feel that many of you have lost hope in yourselves. **Many of you have based your livelihoods on market conditions,** on the circumstances of having the right price or the right monthly traffic count. **The problem with placing your hope in the market is that you place your success in the hands of chance. That is not the way to live your life.**

Your ability to make greater income in today's market is not a matter of chance, but it is a matter of choice. The choices you make each week determine your future—not any other factor.

How we choose to respond to tough markets is what makes the difference between staying afloat and failing. So **we've got to make a choice to change the way we think about sales.** All of this market blaming, all of this "I'll just ride it out" talk has got to stop. We cannot continue to blame bad markets for our failures and then praise ourselves for the sales we win in the good years. **We cannot allow ourselves to be victims of circumstance.** If we do, we put our lives and the lives of those who depend on us on the line.

We need to wake up. We need to have a worth check and realize that we have the power to turn a bad situation around. No matter what market conditions we're facing, we can choose to say, "If I can start performing at a higher level, I will sell more houses."

If we do not choose to reclaim our hope, if we do not choose to take ownership of our success, we will eventually lose the belief that we influence people to buy houses. We'll continue to believe that people only buy houses because of outside factors, and we will continue to be at the market's mercy.

As you read this book, I challenge you to put aside the headlines and everything that the industry has led you to believe about tough markets. **This is your chance to start fresh, to reclaim your hope in yourself and your potential.** If you allow yourself to break free from circumstance, if you commit to creating true, emotional urgency in your sales, you will have the power to be successful regardless of market conditions.

**True urgency
doesn't happen instantly—**

it grows a step at a time.

2

CIRCUMSTANCE *vs.* EMOTION

Which one rules?

There are two types of urgency that you will deal with on a day-to-day basis: *circumstantial urgency* and *emotional urgency.* In order to use these urgencies to their full potential, you need to understand how both types work.

Circumstantial Urgency

Sometimes we have circumstances that create urgency in our sales, and when we do we should make the most of them. These **circumstances could be on the customer's end**. They could have a lease expiring, or maybe they've already sold their current home. Maybe they're being transferred, or they need a new home to accommodate a growing family. Perhaps the customer got a glowing referral from one of your previous buyers. Sometimes there's just a lot of activity going on in the office while the customer is trying to decide what to do.

Circumstantial urgencies could also be on your end.

You could have special short-term incentives or an imminent price increase on the way. You could have more demand than supply. Maybe you're down to the "last one" of what they're looking for, or it's the only one in their time frame.

Market conditions, prices and incentive deals aren't what I'd consider to be "real" reasons for buying a home. **Customers don't purchase a home because of a great deal—they purchase a home because they want to improve their lives.** Even the most jaw-dropping deals will fall through if the customer doesn't believe that your home is the right one for them.

In tough markets, homebuyers know that the circumstances are in their favor. They know that builders want to minimize the market's damage, and they can already see the sweet deals on the horizon—price reductions, free upgrades, even incentives like free furniture will soon be theirs for the taking. **They hope that they can find the home of their dreams, and at the same time benefit from market circumstances.**

So, what's a builder to do? Rev up a new marketing campaign? Splash advertising around town and hope they've got the most attractive deals? Take a financial hit just so they can undercut the competition?

That's the route that most builders take. They believe that by creating circumstantial urgency they will motivate the buyer to purchase. Unfortunately, using circumstantial urgency as an opening tool or your primary selling tool is not going to guarantee a sale. It might help you close a deal, but it's not going to make the customers loyal to your home.

I'm not saying that circumstantial urgency can never be effective. When you do have circumstantial urgencies in your favor, such as an upcoming price increase or more demand than supply, then yes, you can use those circumstances as a selling tool. You definitely want to make sure the customer realizes the consequences of failing to act. However, it's important that you use the circumstance as a secondary selling point, not a primary selling point. Here's why.

What happens when circumstances aren't in your favor? What happens when the market slows down? What happens when your competitors are offering better incentives? What if your customer isn't in a hurry to sell their old house?

To sell value in a tough market you have to stay focused on building true, emotional urgency within each buyer. You have to show them how your homes satisfy their needs better than anyone else's could. **If you do not help customers to fall in love with your homes, if you do not help them to develop a deep, emotional, I-have-to-have-it connection with a home, then there's really no reason they should choose you over the competition if all it comes down to is price.**

Now think about this for a moment: If you're relying on circumstantial urgency to sell your homes, who's calling the shots in the sale? I have some bad news—it's not you. You're letting the customer, the market and all kinds of outside factors determine your results, and that's not how it should be. **You are the leader in your customer relationships.** Your job is to lead your customer through the buying process and to the home that satisfies their needs, wants and dreams. You cannot lead your customer to the final close successfully if you choose to sit in the passenger seat and let them drive.

When we give up our leadership, **when we yield to the idea that "the customer only cares about price," or that "today's market is totally price-driven," we get buyers to make a rational commitment to our deal without**

making an <u>emotional</u> commitment to our home. That is a classic prescription for buyer's remorse, a dysfunctional relationship after contract, and a high likelihood of cancellation. And, you know what? Most of your competitors are banking on circumstances to sell their homes.

If you want to win sales from the competition, you need to step away from this bad habit. You must not rely on circumstantial urgency to sell homes. As the leader in the relationship, **you can make sales even when the circumstances surrounding you are not in your favor.** How do you do that? By tapping into a different kind of urgency: emotional urgency.

Emotional Urgency

Emotional urgency is the desire to improve our lives. It is the most powerful urgency of all, and it occurs when we realize that we can take an action that will make our life better, and that the sooner we take it, the sooner our life will improve. **Emotional urgency lies at the heart of selling in its purest form.**

To understand how emotional urgency develops, let's examine the buying process that takes place in another industry: new car sales.

When you shop for a new car, how does your decision evolve? For many people it evolves like this…

The customer walks into the showroom saying, "I'm just looking." Their old car still runs fine. There are plenty of cars on the lot. Plenty of other dealers are within striking distance. So, how does someone in car sales ever create urgency? One step at a time.

The customer gets into the car and the salesperson explains a few features. As the customer gets more interested in the new car, and becomes more comfortable with the salesperson, the salesperson begins to ask questions about the old car. **There must be *something* about the old car that the customer is dissatisfied with, or else they wouldn't be out shopping.**

Often the urgency to actually buy the new car doesn't even begin until the test drive. This is like the model demonstration and the trip to the site in our business. **The test drive is when the customer becomes emotionally involved in the new car as the experience of enjoying it comes to life.** The salesperson can then tap into the customer's desire to improve his life. They can ask, "How does this compare with your current car?" Before long, they can set up the close by asking, **"Which car would you like to drive home in: this one, or your old one?"**

New home sales works the same way. **True urgency doesn't happen instantly—it grows a step at a time**, and it usually doesn't even begin to develop until the customer wants a particular home. That's when emotional urgency begins to take root and grow.

To build emotional urgency within our customers, we must uncover their intrinsic reasons for wanting a new home, and then help them discover how one of our homes can satisfy their mission to improve their lives. We're not talking about manipulation here. In fact, I know that's probably a concern for you, so we're going to cover that later. But for now, just know that when it comes to building emotional urgency, your goal is to help the customer make a decision with confidence. Keep the primary focus on the home and on their emotional attachment to it. This will increase your chance of making the sale, and at the same time reduce the chance of buyer's remorse.

People are buying homes in today's market. The only question is, who are they buying homes from? They are buying homes from the sales counselors who help them to fall in love with their homes more than with anyone else's.

You are the most important variable in the equation…

You are the X-Factor.

3

The

X-FACTOR

The first step to breaking free from circumstance is to create your strategy for success. You've got to determine where you are now, and then figure out why you're there. Then you can outline what it will take to achieve the success you desire.

Where are we now? Well, we're struggling to make our monthly sales goals. **If we choose not to blame the market, then we've got to uncover the true reason why we're falling short of our goals.**

To uncover the "why" of our situation, I need to show you a math formula. I heard that heavy sigh—I know what most of you are thinking. "A math formula?! I'm in sales and we don't do math." I felt the same way until I figured out this formula. I was the kid in school who would always complain to my math teacher that algebra has no real-world application. That has been true until now. I will do my best to make this section as painless as possible.

You need to look at this sales formula as **a new way of strategic thinking in sales**. It shows you three factors that make your Monthly Sales Goal happen: Average Price, Monthly Traffic and your Conversion Rate.

$$\text{Monthly Sales Goal in Revenue} = \text{Average Price} \times \text{Monthly Traffic} \times \text{Conversion Rate}$$

To understand how these factors impact your success, you need to remember two things about equations. First, just as with any equation, **all factors are dependent upon the other factors**. For example, if you lower your price, you must increase your traffic or your conversion rate in order to reach your revenue goal. Second, **the value on the left side must equal the value on the right side.** Otherwise, the equation is not true. Now let's plug some real-life numbers into this formula so that we can see it in action.

Let's say your monthly sales goal in revenue is $1.2 million. The average price of homes in your community is $300,000. So right away you know that you have to sell four homes to reach your goal. But wait—you only sold one home this month. Before you stress, let's flesh out the rest of the equation. Remember, we don't want to blame the market—we want to uncover the true reason for falling short of our goal.

You check your records and see that your traffic this month was 80. You sold one home, so your conversion rate for the month was one home per 80 customers, or 1/80.

$$\$1.2 \text{ million} = \$300,000 \times 80 \times \frac{1}{80}$$

Now you multiply all three factors on the right side: 300,000 times 80 times 1/80 equals… 300,000.

$$\$1.2 \text{ million} \neq \$300,000$$

Obviously that doesn't equal the left side of your equation, your monthly sales goal of $1.2 million.

To figure out why you're falling short, you've got to balance the equation. What if you lowered your monthly sales goal from $1.2 million to only $300,000? Well, that would harm not just your personal income, but also your company's bottom line. So let's scratch that idea.

Can you lower your price? Will that help you to make more sales? Let's say you lower your price to $250,000. That means you'll have to sell even *more* homes to reach your goal of $1.2 million. **Not a good idea.**

How about increasing your traffic? Well, if it takes 80 units of traffic for you to make just one sale, and you want to make four sales in a month, that means you're going to have to *quadruple* your traffic. **You'll need to find a way to get 320 people to walk through your door each and every month.**

So, grab a pen, and in the margin start writing down everything you can do to increase your traffic from 80 to 320 every month............... Are you writing yet?................. **Come on! Let's go! Your company and your family are depending on you!**

Any ideas yet… ?

You're right—quadrupling traffic and maintaining that pace every month is a ridiculous idea, no matter what kind of market we're in. So you need to turn to your last variable: your conversion rate.

Your conversion rate is only one sale per 80 customers, so right there you've found the "why," the reason you're falling short of your goal. **And here's the good news—your conversion rate is a factor that you have the power to control.**

Taking control of it requires you to make a choice.

In order to reach your monthly sales goal, you can choose to:

1. **Increase your traffic from 80 to 320 every month (and don't make me remind you how much work that is).**

   Or...

2. **Increase your conversion rate.** *Convince three of the other 79 people who walk through your door to choose you.*

Once you've chosen to increase your conversion rate, you need to figure out how you're going to do it. **The key to increasing your conversion rate is creating emotional urgency in your customers.** You must show them how your home and community can satisfy their mission to improve their life.

A person's desire to improve their life has more influence over their buying decision than any other factor. When a customer buys your home, their final decision comes down to more than just market conditions or price. They are choosing the place where they will live, work, play and grow with their family. This strong desire for a home is what leads customers through your doors even in times of market trouble.

Only you, the sales counselor, can tap into this desire and develop the buyer's urgency to purchase. If customers fall in love with your home, they will choose you over the competition. They will purchase regardless of market circumstances. Do you realize what this means? **You are the most important variable in the equation.**

You—not price, not traffic numbers, but you.

You are the X-Factor. You make the sale happen. Your choice to create emotional urgency will create success for you, market-in and market-out. Nothing in life is guaranteed. Unforeseen circumstances can and will affect you. But, you do have to make choices in life, and **all I want you to do is to make the choice that gives you the highest probability that you will succeed.**

You achieve success by choosing to convert more sales from the traffic you have. And how do you do that? You do it by building up the customer's emotional urgency—you want to show them how your home can satisfy their mission to improve their life.

Increasing your conversion rate by creating emotional urgency will give you success even in tough markets, and it will give you unthinkable success in the good ones.

Regardless of what

the headlines say, in the end,

is there really a better time

to improve your life than at

right this very moment?

4

THE SEVEN PHASES

of

EMOTIONAL URGENCY

How come there are some customers who can make a decision to purchase in only two or three days, but there are others who take two or three weeks to make up their minds? Why do some people purchase after seeing only a couple of houses, but others won't make up their minds until they've seen dozens? The answer has to do with how quickly emotional urgency is accomplished.

When it comes to purchasing a home, **emotional urgency develops in seven phases.** How soon someone purchases depends on how quickly he moves through those phases. If we leave customers alone to sell themselves on the home, it's going to take a long time for urgency to develop. They'll wander from community to community looking for the right home, but because no one is helping them, they might pass up the right home without knowing it. This is where our role as the X-Factor comes into play.

We must serve as the catalyst in the customer's decision-making process.

When we lead customers through the Seven Phases of Emotional Urgency, we help them to find their favorite home and site and enable them to make a decision with confidence.

The Seven Phases of Emotional Urgency[1] are:

Phase 1: The customers are unsatisfied with their current home.

Find out exactly what they do not like about their current home. Dig deep to find out their emotional pain points. Don't just find out that they don't like how many bedrooms and baths they have. Instead, ask them what really bothers them about those bedrooms and baths. Is it their size, layout, or their relationship to other rooms in the house? Find out what keeps them up at night. Find out what really frustrates them about their home on an emotional level, not just a logical one.

Phase 2: They want your home more than any other home they have seen, and more than their current home.

Why is this? How does your home make them feel versus the other homes they have seen? What's so special about your home compared to their home and the other homes on the market? Remember, this is not about what *you* feel makes your homes special—it's about what *they* feel makes your homes special.

Phase 3: They believe your home is the best available in your market.

Do your customers feel that they are getting more of what they really want and need out of your homes and community within their financial constraints, and is this value superior to what they would receive from any other builder? Remember, everyone compromises when they buy a home. You don't have to find them

---

1   The Seven Phases of Emotional Urgency have been adapted with permission from concepts in Richard Tiller's *Selling with Momentum (Tiller Marketing Services, Herndon, Virginia, 2003).*

the perfect house, just the perfect house for them at this time in their lives and within the guidelines of what they can afford.

Phase 4: They pick out a favorite home site.

Why is it their favorite? What do they like about it? How are they going to use it? Don't worry if they want the largest lot but can't afford it. The question for them is not "What would your favorite home site be if money were no object?" Instead, you want to remind them of the mission they had when they first walked in the door—the total package of needs, wants and budget. The right question to ask is: "Based on the total package of what you want out of your home and home site, is this home site your favorite?"

Phase 5: They realize that their favorite could be someone else's favorite, too.

Do they feel that if they do not act quickly someone else could buy the home they love? You see, if they believe that they've found the best available home and home site in the market, then it is not a stretch for them to think that someone else would feel the same way. Help them to understand this fact. One way you can do this is by helping them to pick out their second-favorite home and home site. This way they will see that they don't want their *second* favorite home and home site. **What they want is their favorite home and home site—their *first* choice.**

Phase 6: They believe they are in the right place at the right time.

Do your customers feel that there is no better time to buy than right now? In tough markets, there will always be a lot of naysayers who tell your customers not to buy. For example, just look at some of these quotes from the media:

"If you are looking to buy, be careful.
Rising home values are not a sure thing anymore."
—*The Miami Herald*

"A home is where the bad investment is."
—*San Francisco Examiner*

As you can see, the media don't exactly make it easy for you to keep your hopes up. Oh, wait—I forgot to give you the dates for those quotes…

"If you are looking to buy, be careful.
Rising home values are not a sure thing anymore."
—*The Miami Herald, October 25,* **1985**

I'm sure glad that I listened to *The Miami Herald* in 1985 and didn't buy real estate. Man, would I have been sorry.

"A home is where the bad investment is."
—*San Francisco Examiner, November 17,* **1996**

The *San Francisco Examiner* really nailed that one, huh? If people had listened to their advice, they would have missed one of the greatest financial opportunities of the decade.

My reason for giving you these quotes is to show you that if there is bad news out there, then the media are going to find it. So when it comes down to the right time to buy real estate, now is the right time. Not tomorrow, not yesterday, but right this very second.

Regardless of what the headlines say, in the end, is there really a better time to improve your life than at right this very moment?

Phase 7: They realize that the sooner they act, the sooner their lives will improve.

This is the most important urgency phase. This is also one that sometimes is overlooked in new home sales. People buy things to make their lives easier and better. So as you lead customers through the sale, help them answer the following questions for themselves: Why will this house improve their lives? Why will this community improve their lives? Will the home bring their family closer together? Will it bring organization to their lives? How will this home and community make them feel as a person, a parent or a spouse? How will their kids' lives improve?

They might not ask these questions out-loud, but these thoughts are tucked away in their minds somewhere. If you help them to answer these questions, you will help them to realize that the sooner they act, the sooner their lives will improve.

*   *   *

And there you have them—the Seven Phases of Emotional Urgency. If you fulfill these phases when you sell your homes and community, you will be the catalyst that helps the customer's urgency to evolve. **Customers will discover how owning your home will enable them to complete the mission they began when they first walked in your door.** And the best part? You'll have the satisfaction of knowing that you earned that sale. You—not circumstances, not the customer, not the market or the incentives—but *you* were the one who led the customer to their new home.

There are sales out there to be made if you commit to building your customer's emotional urgency. And these sales will propel you past your competition and closer to the success that you desire. **If you want to achieve success in any market, you must mutually accomplish all Seven Phases of Emotional Urgency more than anyone else does.** Turn to the next chapter to see how you can make that happen.

A closing question must
require the customer
to make a decision.

5

MUTUAL ACCOMPLISHMENT

What is it?

In order to execute the Seven Phases of Emotional Urgency successfully, you must complete each phase with all buyers involved. This is called *mutual accomplishment*.

It is easier to describe what mutual accomplishment is by explaining what it is *not*. If the sales counselor accomplishes one of the phases of urgency in his or her mind, without also securing the outward agreement of that accomplishment, then from the customer's perspective the phase has not been accomplished. No emotional commitment has been made.

Mutual accomplishment cannot be achieved with just a nod of the head—it's got to be achieved through a series of verbal agreements between you and all the buyers involved in the purchase.

How do we create it?

The best way to secure a verbal agreement is through asking a closing question related to that urgency phase. The closing question must be one that requires the customer to make a decision. Following are some examples of closing questions that are geared to achieve mutual accomplishment.

Phase 1: The customers are unsatisfied with their current home.

"So, Jim and Mary, you told me you are looking for a home that gives you: a larger living space so that you can have room for your football watching parties; a fourth bedroom for the upcoming arrival of your new baby, Luke, while allowing you to keep your guest room; and you can have a separate room to use as a home office so that you can have quality family time without having to give up your workload. Jim and Mary, does that sound like the kind of home that you are looking for?"

Phase 2: They want your home more than any other home they have seen, and more than their current home.

Summarize Phase 1, and then say, "Based on that information, does this home accomplish what you were looking for in your next home?"

Phase 3: They believe your home is the best available in your market.

"Based on everything that you have seen on the market, does this home accomplish more of what you want and need in a home based upon the money that you want to spend?"

Phase 4: They pick out a favorite home site.

"Based upon the budget that you have created for your next home and home site, will 2255 Waters Edge Lane work for you and your family?"

Phase 5: They realize that their favorite could be someone else's favorite, too.

"Jim and Mary, you told me that the Huntington floor plan would be the best home for you because of x, y and z. You also told me that, of the three home sites we visited, you liked 2255 Waters Edge Lane the best because it was the closest one to the community playground, it had a backyard size that was manageable, and you could watch the sunset from your back porch because of the direction the house would face. Is that right? Do you believe this is the best home and home site combination in the community? Well, Jim and Mary, we see about 15 people per week here in River Park community and they're all looking for their next home. Do you feel there is a good chance that just one of those other 14 people will feel the same way you do about the Huntington Home on 2255 Waters Edge Lane?"

"Yes."

"Well, I do too! So, here are your choices. Choice A is to put an earnest deposit down, and then let's write up a contract to take that home and home site off the market. Or, Choice B is to pick out one of the other two locations that would be your second favorite site for your Huntington home. Which choice would you like to make at this point?"

Phase 6: They believe they are in the right place at the right time.

"If you don't buy here and you don't buy now, what is it that will make you feel that it's the right time to buy?"

Phase 7: They realize that the sooner they act, the sooner their lives will improve.

> "You should not buy a home unless you believe that the home will improve your life. So, do you believe this home will improve your life?"

*　*　*

I hope that these examples have helped you to understand the types of closing questions that will be most effective in reaching mutual accomplishment. These are questions that require a definite response. They require the customer to verbally make a decision and acknowledge that they are aware of the commitment they are making.

If you struggle with being a leader in the salesperson-customer relationship, you may feel uneasy about asking these types of questions. But trust me, customers expect it. They didn't come to the sales office looking for a new best friend—they came because they wanted to find someone who could help them find a home.

Customers expect you to sell!

What happens if we don't have mutual accomplishment?

When a customer comes in to make an offer, and we have not mutually accomplished the Seven Phases of Emotional Urgency, who has the upper hand?

The customer does. Let me explain.

I once coached a sales counselor who was convinced that she had accomplished all of the phases of urgency with a customer. I asked her what would happen if the customer were to come in tomorrow and say that the builder down the street is offering $20k off their homes, and that it's hard to pass up that deal. What would she say to that customer? Immediately she responded, "I'd say, 'Let me call my sales manager to see what we can do.'" I then asked her, "Are you selling from a position of strength at that moment?"

"No," she said.

And I replied, "That is because you have not mutually accomplished the Seven Phases of Emotional Urgency."

Now think about this: **when a customer comes in to make an offer and you** *have* **mutually accomplished the Seven Phases of Emotional Urgency**, who has the position of strength? That's right—**you** are in control of the sale. **The customer has essentially sold themselves on the home and site.** All you have to do is close them and welcome them to the community!

There's one last point about mutual accomplishment that I need to address. You must **ensure that it's been fulfilled for all decision makers involved** in the buying process. When a couple walks in, many times the sales counselor will sell to just one person.

For example, let's say that you're touring Robert and Leslie through a model that you're certain will be their favorite. You walk through each room and help Leslie to make all sorts of decisions about what they want in their next home. She says that the home would provide their two children with their own rooms, and the extra room could become a craft room where she can begin her home business. She is thrilled about that.

Throughout the entire process, Robert remains aloof,

so you continue to involve only Leslie in the conversation, and you make sure that you move her through the Seven Phases of Emotional Urgency. Two hours later, all of the decisions have been made, and the couple decides they want to go home and sleep on it. It seems like the perfect home for them, so you are confident that they're going to sign the contract. You're anticipating victory.

The next afternoon, you begin to wonder why Leslie hasn't called you yet. You were almost certain that she would call last night before the office closed. So, you pick up the phone and give her a ring. Robert answers and you ask him if he and Leslie are ready to come in and sign the contract on their dream home. "No," he answers, "we've decided that we need to spend some more time looking." Wait—you were under the impression that they were ready to buy. You'd accomplished all seven of the phases, right? What's the deal? **Why do they need more time?** You go right out and say to Robert:

> "Yesterday it seemed that this was the perfect home for you. It had everything that you were looking for. What's caused you to want to think about it some more?"

"Well," he replies, "it had everything Leslie was looking for, but I didn't see any rooms that would work for my recording studio. I don't want her to have to give up her craft room, so I guess it's back to the drawing board for us."

Very quickly, you assure Robert that you have another home that would satisfy his needs, and you invite him and Leslie back to take a tour. He accepts, and you give a sigh of relief as you realize that you avoided disaster. Then, you begin to put the pieces together and realize what must have happened. **Once they got**

home, the silent husband became vocal and began disagreeing with the decisions that were made that day. He wanted the extra room so that he could build his own recording studio, but Leslie desperately wanted the extra room so that she could start a business of her own. At that moment the sale was stopped! **If you had only spent time talking to Robert**, uncovering his thoughts and needs for the home, you could have moved him through the phases of urgency. Luckily, in this case, you have that chance again.

The bottom line is, **don't dare believe the old saying that "the wife is the only one who buys the home."** Not today. Not anymore. In today's market, the husband has his own dreams and wishes for this life-changing purchase. If you have completed the Seven Phases of Emotional Urgency with a customer, but for some reason they still have not purchased, the reason is probably the other buyer. Did you accomplish all seven phases with both buyers? Did you close each person individually on the home? You must mutually accomplish the Seven Phases of Emotional Urgency with each decision maker, or else you risk leaving the sale in limbo.

Challenge

I have a challenge for you. For the next week, review the Seven Phases of Emotional Urgency and plan how you will implement what you've learned. Plan and rehearse the questions that you will use to lead your customers through each phase. Then, put your plan into action each day. Keep a brief journal of your experiences and share that journal with your sales manager. At the end of the week you can evaluate how this technique has impacted your sales.

Remember:

People are buying homes in today's market. The only question is, who are they buying homes from? They are buying homes from the sales counselors who are accomplishing more of the Seven Phases of Emotional Urgency than anyone else is.

"When you change the way you look at things,

the things you look at change."

—*Based upon the Heisenberg Uncertainty Principle*

"When you change the way you look at selling, *selling will change.* **When you change the way you look at yourself,** *you will change."*

—*Jason Forrest*

MAINTAINING

Your

POSITION OF STRENGTH

In order to execute the Seven Phases of Emotional Urgency, you must hold a position of strength. **Holding your position of strength means that you accept and execute your role as the leader in the salesperson-customer relationship.** This is a concept we cover in our Leadership Selling® training, so let me briefly explain what this means.

Between the two of you, *you* are the person who knows the most about your homes and your community. You are like an experienced mountain guide who knows every twig, every stone and every fork in the trail. Homebuyers are amateur climbers who need your leadership in order to reach the summit. Without you, they cannot make the journey. Therefore, **you must act as their leader so that they can find the home of their dreams.** If the customer were a first-time mountain climber ready to ascend Mt. Everest, you would be the Sherpa whom they need to lead the way.

It can be difficult to assert your position of strength in tough markets because, when a prospect walks into your sales office for the first time, they have the upper hand and they know it. They hold the position of strength because you're urgent to sell, but they're not urgent to buy—you want to sell them a home more than they want to buy one.

Now think back to the 2004 market. When customers walked through the door in 2004, who had the position of strength? The sales counselor had it because the prospect wanted the home more then the sales counselor wanted to sell them a home.

You might be thinking to yourself, "Hold on a second, cowboy, that's not true—I love to sell to everyone." I am not saying that you don't love selling to everyone. You wouldn't be in this career if you weren't passionate about selling homes. I am talking about simple supply and demand. The reality is that in 2004 you had more demand than you had supply. It was a seller's market.

Buying a home in 2004 was like walking into a toy store during the holidays—customers were eager to improve their lives and they wanted to make sure they got the house of their dreams before someone else snatched it up. Yes, you wanted to sell them a home, but you had to maintain a fair system for choosing the buyers who could buy from you, such as lotteries and waiting lists. Therefore, you couldn't match their level of urgency and excitement until it was certain that you could sell to them. It wasn't anything personal. You just couldn't afford to give up your position of strength and let them persuade you to do anything unethical, such as bump them up on the waiting list or deny another customer the home or site they wanted.

In a troubled market, the atmosphere of your sales office is much different. Buyers don't burst through the door with urgency. Their lack of enthusiasm drains the energy right out of you, so you might not feel eager to talk with them. You might just greet them, hand them a brochure and point them towards the models. This does not make you a bad person. It just proves that, when you allow the customer to hold the position of strength, the sale can take a bad turn.

How can you gain control in a market where there is more supply than demand? What do you do when customers feel like they have all the time in the world to make their decision?

How does a sales counselor sell from a position of strength when it feels like the customers are the ones holding all the cards?

It's very simple: in order to successfully execute the Seven Phases of Emotional Urgency, **you have to find ways to change the position of strength over to your favor.** I know what you're probably thinking at this point. Sell from a position of strength? Find ways to change the position of strength over to my favor? That's kind of manipulative, isn't it? Well, it depends on how you look at it.

There is a difference between manipulation and persuasion. When it comes down to it, you can distinguish them with one word: intent. Your intent and how you execute your position of strength determines if you are crossing the line and moving from pure persuasion to malicious manipulation. Persuaders use their position of strength for the customer's benefit and wellbeing. Manipulators have ulterior motives, and are concerned only with their own wellbeing. Their goal is to coerce the prospect to purchase a home regardless of whether or not it satisfies their needs, wants or budget.

Unfortunately, many sales counselors don't see the difference between persuasion and manipulation. They feel that they are one in the same, so they shy away from persuasion. To avoid coming across as aggressive, pushy and manipulative, they try to become the customer's friend. **They essentially abandon their position of strength and hand it over to the customer.** An example of this would be giving the customer a brochure and sending them to tour the models without you. How can you help the customer to fall in love with your homes if you aren't there to help them appreciate what you have to offer? Taking a customer on a community tour is just one way to exercise your position of strength.

If you struggle with persuasion, you need to change your perception of it. Early in life, I learned that the way I see the world affects how I interpret things. And my perception of the world is created by the experiences of my past. For example, let's say that as a young child you had a terrifying experience on an airplane. You flew through a thunderstorm at night, and the turbulence made you feel as if the plane were going to fall from the sky at any moment.

As an adult, you would probably approach airplanes with an understandable fear. Many others, however, might perceive flying to be a safe and even fun way to travel. They could step into an airplane without giving it a second thought. If you want to be like these people, and rid yourself of the fear of flying, you will have to work on undoing the damage from your past experiences and change your perception of flying. That's not an easy task, but with the right support and education, it certainly is doable.

Like the young child on the nerve-wracking flight, many new home salespeople have had negative experiences with sales in their past. Maybe they tagged along with their father to the used car lot and heard his speech that salespeople are con-artists whose goal is to rip you off. Or, perhaps they've dealt with a lot of rude, pushy telemarketers. Whatever the case, some of us have had encounters with manipulative people, and we've sworn that we would never, ever behave that way towards our customers.

If this is you, if you are fearful that maintaining a position of strength will scare away your customers, I challenge you to change your perception of persuasion and see it for the positive tool that it is.

When you engage in persuasion, you are building a case for your product so that the customer may make an informed purchase decision. There is nothing unethical about it. You uncover the customer's needs and wants, provide the customer with solid, honest information about the homes that satisfy those needs and wants, get their feedback, answer their questions, and then invite them to close on their favorite home. No games. **No tricks.** If you truly love your homes and are proud of your community, you will have no need to engage in coercion or underhanded sales strategies.

If you're concerned that you're being manipulative, examine your intent and determine whose interests you have in mind. **If you're looking out for the customer, you're engaging in persuasion and you're good to go.** If you only care about your own wellbeing, you need to reevaluate your priorities and seek a change of heart.

What about incentives?

In troubled markets, customers are going to test you to see if you'll give up your position of strength. Within minutes of your greeting they will ask you questions about incentives and the deals you can give them.

If your incentives are being offered publicly, such as in your advertising or in your handouts, this means your incentives are intended to be offered as part of your basic price. In other words, you may use these incentive circumstances as a selling tool and share them when you discuss price.

However, **if the incentives are not advertised, you should treat them as a negotiating tool, not as an opening or selling tool.** Many salespeople tend to give away negotiating incentives too early, jumping right to them at the same time they're giving the price. Why? They hope this will create urgency and reduce their chances of losing a sale. Can this strategy work? I can't say "absolutely never," but I will say that it's not your best bet for winning the sale.

When you cut straight to the incentives, you might think you're adding emotional urgency to the equation, but you're not. **You're actually cutting down the value of the incentives and your homes.** You're telling the customer that the reason they should buy your home is to get an incentive. That's it. Not because you have the community and homes that will improve their lives. Not because your homes are better than the competition's. You're telling the customer that they need to buy because they'll get something for free. Eventually, those once-attractive incentives will become old news, and you'll have a cancellation on your hands unless the customer loves your home more than anyone else's. **The larger a factor an incentive is in a customer's decision to buy, the more likely they will be to cancel.**

When you skip emotional urgency and cut straight to price talks, you not only give up your position of strength, but you also throw the customer's best interests under the bus. The customer is so caught up in circumstance, in the deals and incentives, that they forget their main mission: to find the home that best suits their needs, wants and dreams. As the leader in the relationship, it is your responsibility to hold them accountable to fulfilling their mission. They're trusting that you will find the right home for them and you cannot let them down.

Therefore, **you must remember to exercise your position of strength by using circumstantial urgency not as a primary selling tool, but as your closing tool.** This means that instead of talking about price right away, you need to focus on helping the customer to fall in love with the home that will fulfill their mission.

If you're beginning a conversation with a customer and they ask you about incentives and deals straight away, you can reply:

> "It varies depending on several factors: which home and site you choose; how far along the home is; how many special features have already been pre-selected; and how soon you can move. If you see a home you really like, I'll be able to give you better information about our incentives once I know what I have to work with."

You might perceive this strategy as giving the customer the run-a-round. But really, all you're doing is upholding the value of your homes, and **you're helping the customer to see the real value of the incentive**. Let me give you an illustration to show you what I mean.

Have you ever walked into a clothing store and been ambushed by the salesperson who rattles off the day's specials? They say something such as, "Today only, all of the jeans on the clearance table are half-off." You walk over to the clearance table and look through them, and find a pair that looks OK. On sale, they're only $50. You try them on, and then carry them around the store for a few minutes while you look at other items. After a while, you think to yourself, "I don't really like these jeans that much… maybe I don't want them. Why would I spend $50 on something I'm not that crazy about?" So you put them back and walk out.

Now imagine that you're walking into a different department store and are greeted by a helpful salesperson. She asks you a couple of questions, narrows down the jeans that will fit you best, and presents you with three pairs to try on. They all fit well enough, but one pair fits perfectly. You know you look great in them. But when you reach for the price tag, you realize that it's missing. You call out to the salesperson, "How much are these?" She says that normally they are $150, but today they are 15% off. How cool is that? You find the perfect pair of jeans, and they're on sale. That seals the deal for you.

Imagine how a customer will feel when they've fallen in love with a home, and then discover that they're going to get a great grand-opening deal. It's the icing on the cake for them. Or, imagine if they've found their dream home and then realize that you only have one lot left where it will fit.

If you've led a customer through the Seven Phases of Emotional Urgency, and have shown them the value in the home and community, and what they can do for their lives, circumstantial urgency can be your closing tool that wins the sale.

Most people give up when
they fail one time.
Successful people fail, debrief,
realign, and try again.

7

SAY "GOODBYE"

to

GUESSWORK

Each week in sales offices all across the nation, sales managers ask their teams, **"How many sales are you going to make this week?"** and sales counselors have to come up with a number. When this happens to you, what goes through your mind? Maybe something like this…

> "Let's see… the Joneses have been here five times in the past week. So I'll bet they're going to buy. And the Martins have been here eight times this month—this has got to be the week that they're ready to buy."

What's wrong with that strategy? Well, maybe you're not the only community those buyers have visited. Maybe the reason they haven't made a decision is because they don't know if they've found the right home yet.

Here's another thought process that you might go through:

> "Well, I can't say 'zero'… but I don't want to make any promises I can't keep… so I'll play it safe and say 'one.'"

Do you remember the good news that I gave you at the beginning of this book? **You don't have to fumble for an answer— you can know it.** When you follow the process of creating emotional urgency, **you can look at the list of seven**

phases and pinpoint where each customer stands.
Therefore, when your manager asks you how many sales you're going to make, you can have a real answer ready.

When we lead customers through the Seven Phases of Emotional Urgency, we move them through *The Sales Funnel*.

The Sales Funnel

Monthly Traffic: _____

The Seven Phases of Emotional Urgency

1
The customers are unsatisfied with their current home.

2
They want your home more than any other home they have seen, and more than their current home.

3
They believe your home is the best available in your market.

4
They pick out a favorite home site.

5
They realize that their favorite could be someone else's favorite, too.

6
They believe they are in the right place at the right time.

7
They realize that the sooner they act, the sooner their lives will improve.

Current Net Sales Per Month: _____

At the top of the diagram, you write down your monthly traffic. This represents your prospects, the number of people who are entering the funnel. When you have successfully moved a customer through the Seven Phases of Emotional Urgency, they will exit the funnel as a buyer. So at the bottom of the Sales Funnel you will write down your net sales for the month. Unless you are the King or Queen of new home sales and your conversion rate is 100%, this number will be lower than your monthly traffic.

So, what happened to the rest of your prospects? Are they lost? No—they are just trapped somewhere in the funnel. They are stuck in one of the urgency phases. Your goal is to determine which prospects are ready to be moved out of the funnel, and then use the following strategy—the Top 10 Prospect Report—to get them out.

Top 10 Prospect Report

Step 1: Identify your Top 10 best prospects and separate them from the rest of your prospects.

At this point, work with prospects you know can qualify. The prospects that will be financially challenged or at risk of sitting on the qualifying fence will go onto a separate pile.

Lets say you've collected 50 prospect cards over the last few months. Your first task is to go through and divide them solely based upon their income, and whether or not they have enough equity in their current home to be able to sell it in today's market. These people are your leads. The others are not your leads.

I know there will be some people in the discard pile who you want to help. I'm not saying that you shouldn't help them. Just don't help them yet. So many times I've coached sales counselors who want to spend more time than they should on people who can't qualify. **Ironically, the people who can't qualify are often the ones who aggressively pursue the sales counselor.** You know what I mean—a customer comes in and approaches you asking for information about how they can get into one of your homes. You immediately turn into the lifeline that they're looking for as you try to find them all sorts of special financing packages to make it happen.

And then what happens? You can't find them any magical financing packages, so you have to give them their earnest money back. **You then look at your calendar and realize that you have wasted many hours of physical and emotional time on that buyer.** At the same time, the only other customers who have walked through the door have been "just looking," aloof, a little rude or just not urgent to buy. You don't want to be pushy, so you leave them alone and wait for whom you think are the more serious buyers. This harmful mindset threatens to rob you of your sales.

Be Aware of the Wall Huggers

One of my clients recently told me a story about a time he walked into a model home and was completely avoided by the sales counselor. (Yes, he can qualify. Actually, he can probably afford to buy more than one home at a time, if you know what I mean.) He walked into the office, and the sales counselor got up, greeted him and asked how she could help. He said he came to see the models and she said, "OK, the models are that way—please take your time and enjoy the community." After about 20 minutes of touring the models by himself, he came back to the sales office. The sales counselor approached him and asked if he had any questions. He said that he would like to see a brochure. She gave him one; he looked it over, said thanks, and left.

I asked him, "Were you not in the market for a new home?" He said, "I was in the market for a new home… she just didn't think that I was, I guess."

Do you see what happened? The sales counselor expected *him* to be the one who would lead the conversation. The sales counselor expected him to walk in the door with urgency and show interest before she started selling.

This is a common mistake. **We can become so used to buyers performing for us that, when they don't, we think they aren't really buyers.** So here is my advice: change the filter you use to size up the "real" buyers. From now on, every time you encounter a Wall Hugger, engage them! That's the moment when you need to "turn it on" and really sell. Remember, buyers are not supposed to be urgent in tough markets. You have to help build their urgency.

Step 2: Go through the Seven Phases of Emotional Urgency to see if each particular one has been mutually accomplished.

Write out specifics next to each phase and detail *how* it was mutually accomplished. (Make sure you have accomplished each phase for all decision-makers involved.) Remember, it does not matter if you accomplish the phase in *your* eyes; what matters is that the customer believes and has agreed that the phase has been accomplished in *their* eyes.

Step 3: Add up how many of the seven phases you have accomplished with each prospect and write that number on the report.

Step 4: Identify the next phase that needs to be accomplished with each prospect.

Step 5: Identify specific steps that will be taken to accomplish the next phase with each prospect.

Always ask yourself, "What is the next step to get this prospect closer to buying?" Don't worry about how to convince them to buy. Just focus on the logical next step. Once you accomplish that step, then focus on the next step. Do this until all of the steps are accomplished and the sale has been made.

Step 6: Role-play specific steps to improve proficiency.

> "Amateurs practice until they get it right.
> Professionals practice until they can't get it wrong."
> —*Unknown*

My first job out of college was serving as a Financial Advisor at a large investment management company. I essentially made my living by managing my clients' money. The only problem with this concept is that you need clients before you can manage their money. So, every single workday we were required to make 100 cold calls. We were given lists of people who had the kind of net worth that would make them viable prospects for our services.

The cold calling started every day at 7:30 a.m. so that we could catch people at home or as they arrived at work. But, before we could start calling, we had to come together and role-play at 7:00

a.m. At the time I hated nothing more than beginning my day with a role-play exercise. But, as I look back on the experience, I now believe there was nothing more valuable that I could have been doing at 7:00 a.m. You see, our sales manager knew that **these leads were valuable. They were too valuable for us to take the risk of botching them while our brains were still waking up.** Before we even dialed the phone we needed to get back into the groove of making our calls.

For this reason, I now believe that role-playing is one of the best ways to get us firing on all cylinders. Don't be afraid of it. Don't view it from a performance evaluation perspective. Instead, view it as a coaching session, an opportunity for self-improvement, and don't worry about being evaluated by your boss. That's not the point of role-play.

The point of role-play is for you to practice your skills in front of your team the same way an athlete would practice in front of his or her coach. Imagine if Tiger Woods said, "I don't want my coach or any of the other players to watch me," and only wanted to practice alone. That would be silly, right? He wants to practice with his coach and in front of his peers so that he'll do better when it's show time.

When you role-play, you are using your coach and your teammates for practice and feedback so that, when it really matters, you'll be at the top of your game.

Step 7: Execute.

When you're ready to start calling your Top 10 Prospects, don't worry about contacting all of them right away. Just choose three or four at a time to focus on, and then execute what you've rehearsed in Steps 5 and 6.

> "Execution is what separates the 'knowers' from the 'doers.'"
> —Doug Bauer, COO of William Lyon Homes

Step 8: Debrief and realign.

I believe most people give up when they fail one time. I don't know if it's due to fear, intimidation or insecurity—all I know is that they give up. You have gone so far by trying just one time, so why stop now? **Successful people are the ones who debrief, realign, and try again.**

To debrief, share your follow-up experiences with your coach and/or the other sales counselors. Did you succeed? Did you fail? Did you get in touch with the customer? If not, did you leave a message? If you left a message, then what did the message say?

Also use your debriefing time to learn from other sales counselors. **One of the quickest ways to be successful is to practice the techniques of those who have already achieved success.** Make sure you pay special attention to what worked and what didn't work for others. Don't be afraid to ask questions.

Once you've shared your experiences and received feedback, then it's time to realign. Decide if you are going to adopt a different approach that might be more effective than your last one.

> Most people give up when they fail one time.
> Successful people fail, debrief, realign, and try again.

My wife and I once attended a party with some friends of ours who have a 4-year-old daughter named Matti. In the middle of the party, Matti fell on the tile floor. Immediately, her eyes searched frantically for her father. Without missing a beat, he began to brush his fingertips against his knees, and then said encouragingly, **"Dust yourself off and keep on going."** Matti then got up, dusted her knees like her daddy did, and then trotted off without one tear shed. Amazing. Matti is being taught at a very young age that **failure is going to happen, so you might as well embrace it and move on.**

Here is my advice: be Matti. Dust yourself off, and keep on going.

Step 9: Repeat steps 6-8.

Once you've completed your follow-up with your first set of prospects, start over by choosing three more buyers on your list and then repeat Steps 6-8. **Remember, your goal in this process is not to close them on a contract over the phone. Your goal is to just accomplish the next urgency phase.** Don't put so much pressure on yourself. Just focus on the next step. Once you have accomplished that step, then go to the next step. Keep putting one foot in front of the other. If you are committed to this process, your skills will improve and you'll have the potential to move customers through the funnel quickly, reducing their decision-making time from weeks to just a matter of days.

You are the catalyst for a customer's decision-making process.

If you are strategic about moving customers through the Seven Phases of Emotional Urgency, you will know how many sales you can bank on this month. You will rid yourself of guesswork. You will no longer have to depend upon the market for your success.

Remember:

People are buying homes in today's market. The only question is, whom are they buying from? They are buying from the sales counselors who separate themselves from the rest by believing, thinking, feeling, acting and executing their sales process differently.

Now, go and be the one buyers want to buy from.

… if after reading this book

you do not choose to apply

what you've learned,

then you will be no different

from those who have not read it.

8

Your

NEW BEGINNING

My entire life revolved around football.

From the time I was a little boy I obsessed over it. I played the sport religiously. But as I got older, I realized that being associated with football isn't always a positive thing. Yes, there's the upside of being the athlete, and being recognized by others. But you also get labeled as the "dumb jock." I identified and accepted this paradigm on both sides—I happily accepted the good and didn't do anything to fight the bad. That worked for me for a while, but eventually it got old.

By the time I left home for college, I was tired of being the dumb jock. I wanted to change. I talked to my dad about my frustrations and he gave me some valuable advice: just be different. He said, "If you want to be an academic, start acting like one. Hang around academics and copy what they do—learn their good habits. Once you do that, you will start to become one."

Taking his advice, I went to Texas Christian University and decided to room with academics. Matt Baade was my freshman year roommate, and he read a ton of books. Actually, he wouldn't just read them—he would study them. By the time Matt was finished with a book, it would be covered in highlights, filled with notes in the margins, and dog-eared to remind him of the pages that were of most importance to him.

I remember asking him one night, **"Matt why do you read so much?"** He replied with words that have since changed my life.

He said, **"My mother told me when I was younger that those who don't read are no better off than those who can't read."**

Do you see how powerful that statement is?

It means that every person who has been given the gift of literacy, yet chooses not to use it, is illiterate by choice! Just the same, there are a lot of people out there who go through life powerless, letting their life be controlled by circumstance, and they don't know how to change. **But you are different.** You have been given the answers. You have learned how to reclaim your hope and control of your life.

However, if after reading this book you do not choose to apply what you've learned, then you will be no different from those who have not read it. You will be no different from the person you were the moment before you opened the cover. You will have given up your power to change.

Your ability to make greater income in any market is not a matter of chance, but it is a matter of choice.

The choices you make starting **RIGHT NOW** will decide your future—not any other factor. So make your first choice today—decide that you want to take ownership of your success.

I know it won't be easy. It was difficult for me to leave my bad habits behind, to make myself do the right things for the sake of my education. But I made it through by believing in myself and by desiring success more than I desired my old way of life. You have the power to do the same.

Today is your chance to make a fresh start, to reclaim your hope in yourself and to become the successful sales counselor you know you can be.

9

Your

NEXT STEPS

Time and again in this book I said that a person's desire to improve their life has more influence over their buying decision than any other factor. Likewise, **your desire to improve your <u>own life</u> has more influence over your success than any other factor.** Your desire for success is stronger than any market situation. It's more powerful than any circumstance. It's what will drive you to improve your performance in spite of the naysayers who encourage you to "just ride out" the tough markets.

But before you start to make changes and work on your skills, you've got to make sure you're ready. Trust me on this. If you do not change your mindset first, you will not be able to stick to the changes you make in your sales process.

You have to change WHY you sell BEFORE you càn change HOW you sell.

I wrote this book to help you work on the "why." **Sales Counselors are in the business of improving people's lives.** Once you believe that, you will be ready to change how you sell.

I've also written this book to give you one piece of the "how." I've shown you how creating urgency can increase your conversion rate even in times of market trouble. This is one concept that will give you a good start on your road to success. But, what will your next step be? What will you do after you've mastered urgency?

You've probably realized by now that learning the "how" part does not happen overnight. Improving the skills to lead your customers through the Seven Phases of Emotional Urgency takes diligence. Therefore, when you work on changing how you sell, you must seek out resources that will give you **real solutions, not quick-fixes**. Those kinds of resources probably won't appeal to you, anyway; because if you believe that you are in the business of improving people's lives, then you won't want to engage in training that's based on manipulation and gimmicks. So let me give you a couple of recommendations to get you started.

One book that I recommend is Jeff Shore's *Tough Market New Home Sales,* which was released in January 2008.

One training program that I recommend is Leadership Selling®. It is the most in-depth training curriculum out there, and will equip you with the complete skill set that you need in order to maximize the power of emotional urgency. This training is centered upon the principle that customers need, and want, to buy from leaders. By our definition, a leader is person you will follow to a place that you would not go on your own.

In tough markets, customers need someone to take them where they cannot and do not want go on their own. They need sales counselors who can lead them to a decision with confidence and enthusiasm, in spite of all the naysayers out there who say they should wait, or not buy. We've created Leadership Selling® to show you how to be that leader, to be the person who can lead customers on their mission to improve their lives, and who can accomplish it better than anyone else can.

As you prepare to close this book, I want you to consider the next steps that you are going to take. If you set this book aside, and do not make a conscious decision to implement the things you have learned, then this book will have been nothing but education. Education alone does not transform lives—application does. I challenge you to take out a pen, and to write down what your next steps will be. Make your choice, **decide what you will do** *today* to begin creating emotional urgency in your customers.

Your destiny is now in your hands.

The choice is yours.

Now become the sales professional you know you need to be.

About *the* Author

Jason grew up under the influence of his father, a business owner and professional salesperson, his mother, a persuasive speaking professor, and Zig Ziglar, his Sunday school teacher and world famous salesperson and motivational speaker. He was an All-State football player in high school, and graduated with a degree in psychology and an MBA in marketing. He went on to sell financial services and real estate, then rose to become the National Director of Sales Development for MDC Holdings/Richmond American Homes. These influences and experiences shaped Jason into who he is today: a salesperson first, a trainer on a mission, a national speaker, and a coach who pushes sales organizations to become the best version of themselves. Jason is the President of Shore Forrest Sales Strategies, providing the industry's best coaching and training services for homebuilding companies around North America.

Selling: The Forrest Dynasty

Jason Forrest is a salesperson first and foremost, and understands sales by selling rather than observing. Jason comes from a line of salespeople, and sold his first diamond at eight years old in his father's jewelry store. At family reunions, they tell sales stories. It's the Forrest dynasty. Unlike some sales trainers who are performers or orators first, and salespeople second (if at all), Jason is a salesperson to the core.

Key Accomplishments

Jason is the author of *Creating Urgency in a Non-Urgent Housing Market* and *40 Day Sales Dare for New Home Sales*. Together with Jeff Shore, he is the co-creator of Leadership Selling® and Leadership Selling® for Coaches, a year-long blended-learning training curriculum for new home sales.

Jason's Mission:
To redefine the purpose of today's salespeople.

Jason's Beliefs

- Buyers don't react negatively to selling or to salespeople in general. Buyers react negatively to dishonesty, unhelpfulness, and/or boring behaviors that salespeople sometimes project.
- There are two types of salespeople: those who participate in the process, and those who influence it.
- A person's desire to improve their life has more influence over their buying decision than any other factor. A salesperson has the capability to influence that desire.

Connect with Jason online:

LinkedIn®:   www.linkedin.com/in/jasonforrest

Twitter™:   www.twitter.com/jforrestspeaker

YouTube™:   www.youtube.com/jasonforrest

Email: jason@shoreforrest.com

Websites: www.JasonForrestSpeaker.com
www.ShoreForrest.com

SHORE **sf** FORREST

YOUR SALES STRATEGY PARTNER

Real-World Sales Strategies.
Real-World Results.

Shore Forrest Sales Strategies is all about real-world approaches leading to real-world results. We are about transforming homebuilding companies into sales-driven organizations.

From training, to coaching, to staffing, to overall strategy — if it has to do with sales, we are the contemporary experts. Contact us today. We'll be happy to show you how we can help increase your profitability in a matter of days.

Jeff Shore, Founder & CEO

Jason Forrest, President

www.ShoreForrest.com
530.269.1045

Ordering *and* Resource Information

To order additional copies of *Creating Urgency in a Non-Urgent Housing Market*, please visit www.shoreforrest.com and click on "Products."

For orders of ten or more, please call 817-886-0018.

> 1 copy...$13.95
>
> Bulk orders, 10 or more........................$9.95/ea

Contact us at info@shoreforrest.com for more information about the resources mentioned in this book, or to learn how to:

- Invite Jason Forrest to give a keynote on *Creating Urgency in a Non-Urgent Housing Market*

- Inquire about Shore Forrest's training and consulting services, including Leadership Selling®

Become a Student of

CREATING URGENCY
UNIVERSITY

Jason Forrest has created a triple-threat approach to increase your sales through this powerful **five-week, live, interactive video coaching program**, based upon his book *Creating Urgency in a Non-Urgent Housing Market*. Your live conference* will include Jason's customized strategies to target your personal selling obstacles, real-life activities that you can apply with your next customer, and motivation to keep you moving forward. Change your life by following Jason's triple-threat approach to success: Self, Science, and Sweat.

– SELF –
Learn how to change your behaviors to reach your sales goals.

– SCIENCE –
A step-by-step process to increase your sales productivity.

– SWEAT –
Do what it takes to create some serious urgency with your customers.

Learn more, and watch a sample coaching session at
www.CreatingUrgency.com!

*You do not need a web cam in order to participate; you need only an internet connection and your phone. You may also participate via phone only. For more information, please visit www.CreatingUrgency.com.

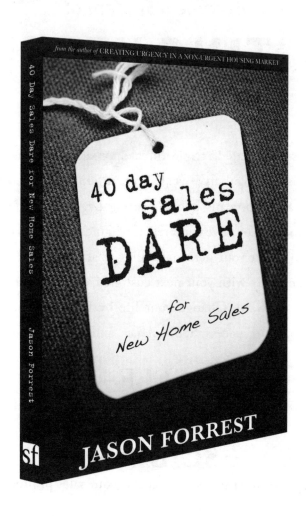

Jason Forrest dares you to explode your career and your income.

www.40DaySalesDare.com

LEADERSHIP SELLING®

Leadership Selling® is not just a seminar—it's a three-level system, taking salespeople to a higher level of skill than is possible with a typical one-day event. Each level consists of weekly lessons, to include:

Education
through weekly, interactive 8-minute videos
and sample sales scripts.

Experiential Learning
through 'Real Play' and weekly assignments in the
Leadership Selling® Handbook.

Group Discussion with Jason Forrest
to review experiences from using
the specific sales techniques.

Management Coaching with Jason Forrest
to equip leaders with the necessary behaviors
and attitudes for coaching successfully.

Watch Informational Videos at
www.LeadershipSelling.com

**40 Day Sales Dare
for New Home Sales**
Jason Forrest

Tough Market New Home Sales
Jeff Shore

Deal With It!
Jeff Shore

Make your purchase at
www.ShoreForrest.com

Outstanding Sales Meetings
Jeff Shore

Tell Us Your Story

Were you impacted by this book? After applying its principles, have you had any "a-ha" moments or exciting experiences that you would like to share?

We at Shore Forrest are passionate about helping sales professionals transform the way they sell and the way they live. If you have a success story, we'd love to hear it!

Send your success stories to:
info@shoreforrest.com